TRUMPET

BIG BOOK *of* DISNEY SONGS

T0039576

Available for
FLUTE, CLARINET, ALTO SAX, TENOR SAX, TRUMPET,
HORN, TROMBONE, VIOLIN, VIOLA, CELLO

ISBN 978-1-4584-1135-8

Walt Disney Music Company
Wonderland Music Company, Inc.

DISTRIBUTED BY

7777 W. BLUEMOUND RD. P.O. BOX 13819 MILWAUKEE, WI 53213

In Australia Contact:
Hal Leonard Australia Pty. Ltd.
4 Lentara Court
Cheltenham, Victoria, 3192 Australia
Email: ausadmin@halleonard.com.au

Visit Hal Leonard Online at
www.halleonard.com

CONTENTS

ALICE IN WONDERLAND

TRUMPET

from Walt Disney's ALICE IN WONDERLAND

Words by BOB HILLIARD
Music by SAMMY FAIN

THE BALLAD OF DAVY CROCKETT

from Walt Disney's DAVY CROCKETT

Words by TOM BLACKBURN
Music by GEORGE BRUNS

BE OUR GUEST

from Walt Disney's BEAUTY AND THE BEAST

Lyrics by HOWARD ASHMAN
Music by ALAN MENKEN

TRUMPET

THE BARE NECESSITIES

from Walt Disney's THE JUNGLE BOOK

Words and Music by
TERRY GILKYSON

BEAUTY AND THE BEAST

TRUMPET

from Walt Disney's BEAUTY AND THE BEAST

Lyrics by HOWARD ASHMAN
Music by ALAN MENKEN

TRUMPET

BELLA NOTTE

(This Is the Night)

from Walt Disney's LADY AND THE TRAMP

Words and Music by PEGGY LEE
and SONNY BURKE

BIBBIDI-BOBBIDI-BOO

(The Magic Song)

from Walt Disney's CINDERELLA

Words by JERRY LIVINGSTON
Music by MACK DAVID and AL HOFFMAN

CRUELLA DE VIL

from Walt Disney's 101 DALMATIANS

Words and Music by
MEL LEVEN

BREAKING FREE

TRUMPET

from the Disney Channel Original Movie HIGH SCHOOL MUSICAL

Words and Music by
JAMIE HOUSTON

BEST OF FRIENDS

from Walt Disney's THE FOX AND THE HOUND

TRUMPET

Words by STAN FIDEL
Music by RICHARD JOHNSTON

CAN YOU FEEL THE LOVE TONIGHT

TRUMPET

from Walt Disney Pictures' THE LION KING

Music by ELTON JOHN
Lyrics by TIM RICE

CANDLE ON THE WATER

TRUMPET

from Walt Disney's PETE'S DRAGON

Words and Music by AL KASHA
and JOEL HIRSCHHORN

CHIM CHIM CHER-EE

TRUMPET

from Walt Disney's MARY POPPINS

Words and Music by RICHARD M. SHERMAN
and ROBERT B. SHERMAN

COLORS OF THE WIND

TRUMPET

from Walt Disney's POCAHONTAS

Music by ALAN MENKEN
Lyrics by STEPHEN SCHWARTZ

A DREAM IS A WISH YOUR HEART MAKES

from Walt Disney's CINDERELLA

Words and Music by MACK DAVID,
AL HOFFMAN and JERRY LIVINGSTON

CIRCLE OF LIFE

TRUMPET

from Walt Disney Pictures' THE LION KING

Music by ELTON JOHN
Lyrics by TIM RICE

GO THE DISTANCE

TRUMPET

from Walt Disney Pictures' HERCULES

Music by ALAN MENKEN
Lyrics by DAVID ZIPPEL

FRIEND LIKE ME

TRUMPET

from Walt Disney's ALADDIN

Lyrics by HOWARD ASHMAN
Music by ALAN MENKEN

GOD HELP THE OUTCASTS

TRUMPET

from Walt Disney's THE HUNCHBACK OF NOTRE DAME

Music by ALAN MENKEN
Lyrics by STEPHEN SCHWARTZ

HOW D'YE DO AND SHAKE HANDS

from Walt Disney's ALICE IN WONDERLAND

Words by CY COBEN
Music by OLIVER WALLACE

HAKUNA MATATA

TRUMPET

from Walt Disney Pictures' THE LION KING

Music by ELTON JOHN
Lyrics by TIM RICE

HE'S A TRAMP

from Walt Disney's LADY AND THE TRAMP

Words and Music by PEGGY LEE
and SONNY BURKE

I JUST CAN'T WAIT TO BE KING

from Walt Disney Pictures' THE LION KING

TRUMPET

Music by ELTON JOHN
Lyrics by TIM RICE

I'M LATE

from Walt Disney's ALICE IN WONDERLAND

Words by BOB HILLIARD
Music by SAMMY FAIN

TRUMPET

IF I NEVER KNEW YOU

(Love Theme from POCAHONTAS)

from Walt Disney's POCAHONTAS

Music by ALAN MENKEN
Lyrics by STEPHEN SCHWARTZ

IT'S A SMALL WORLD

TRUMPET

from Disneyland Resort® and Magic Kingdom® Park

Words and Music by RICHARD M. SHERMAN
and ROBERT B. SHERMAN

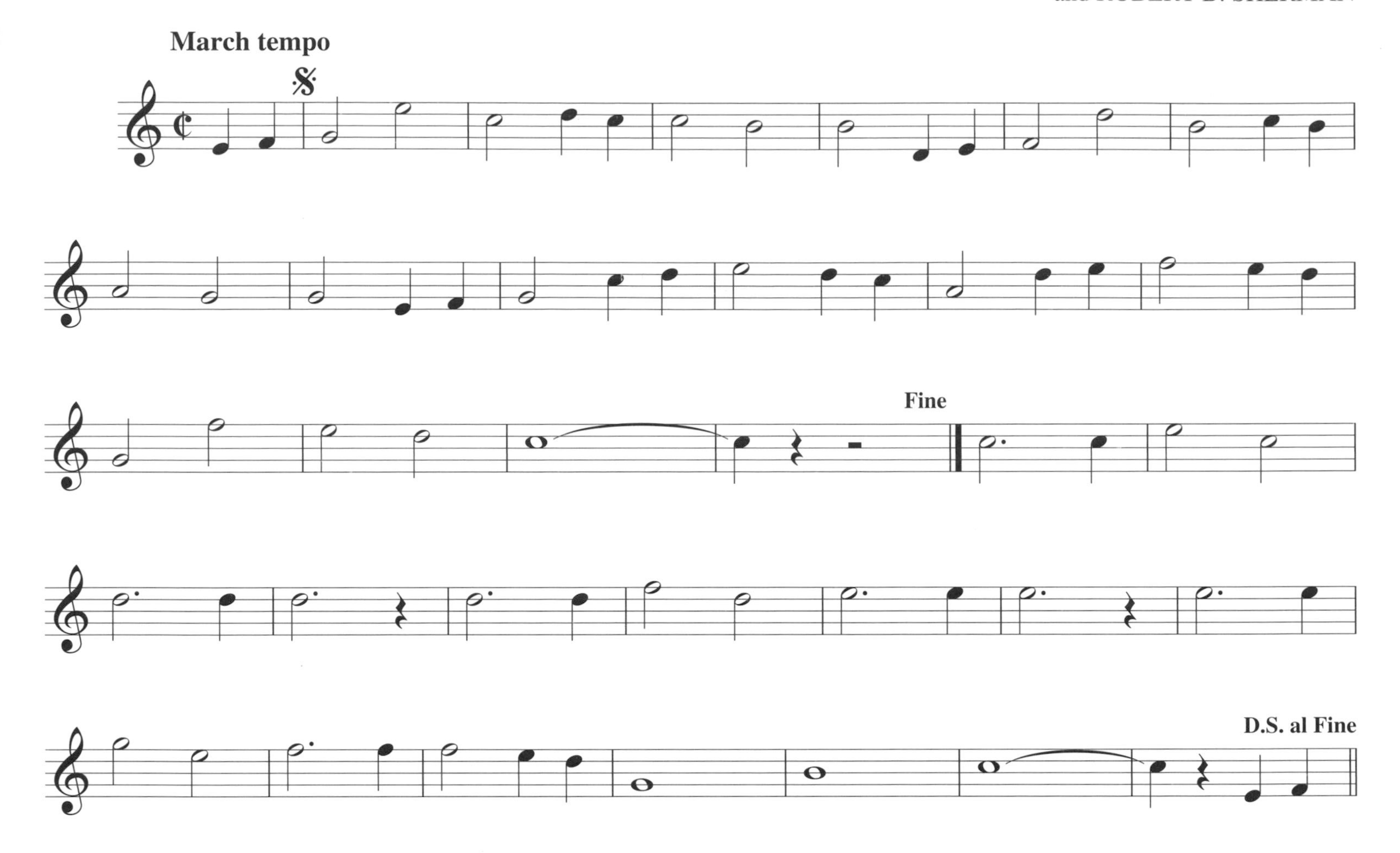

LAVENDER BLUE

(Dilly Dilly)

from Walt Disney's SO DEAR TO MY HEART

Words by LARRY MOREY
Music by ELIOT DANIEL

LET'S GET TOGETHER

from Walt Disney Pictures' THE PARENT TRAP

Words and Music by RICHARD M. SHERMAN
and ROBERT B. SHERMAN

TRUMPET

LET'S GO FLY A KITE

from Walt Disney's MARY POPPINS

Words and Music by RICHARD M. SHERMAN
and ROBERT B. SHERMAN

MY FUNNY FRIEND AND ME

from Walt Disney Pictures' THE EMPEROR'S NEW GROOVE

Lyrics by STING
Music by STING and DAVID HARTLEY

TRUMPET

LITTLE APRIL SHOWER

from Walt Disney's BAMBI

Words by LARRY MOREY
Music by FRANK CHURCHILL

THE LORD IS GOOD TO ME

from Walt Disney's MELODY TIME
from Walt Disney's JOHNNY APPLESEED

Words and Music by KIM GANNON
and WALTER KENT

MICKEY MOUSE MARCH

from Walt Disney's THE MICKEY MOUSE CLUB

Words and Music by
JIMMIE DODD

KISS THE GIRL

TRUMPET

from Walt Disney's THE LITTLE MERMAID

Music by ALAN MENKEN
Lyrics by HOWARD ASHMAN

NEVER SMILE AT A CROCODILE

TRUMPET

from Walt Disney's PETER PAN

Words by JACK LAWRENCE
Music by FRANK CHURCHILL

PART OF YOUR WORLD

from Walt Disney's THE LITTLE MERMAID

TRUMPET

Music by ALAN MENKEN
Lyrics by HOWARD ASHMAN

TRUMPET

ONCE UPON A DREAM

from Walt Disney's SLEEPING BEAUTY

Words and Music by SAMMY FAIN
and JACK LAWRENCE
Adapted from a Theme by Tchaikovsky

REFLECTION

from Walt Disney Pictures' MULAN

Music by MATTHEW WILDER
Lyrics by DAVID ZIPPEL

1.
2., 3.
To Coda
D.S. al Coda
(take 2nd ending)
CODA

A PIRATE'S LIFE

from Walt Disney's PETER PAN

TRUMPET

Words by ED PENNER
Music by OLIVER WALLACE

SCALES AND ARPEGGIOS

from Walt Disney's THE ARISTOCATS

Words and Music by RICHARD M. SHERMAN
and ROBERT B. SHERMAN

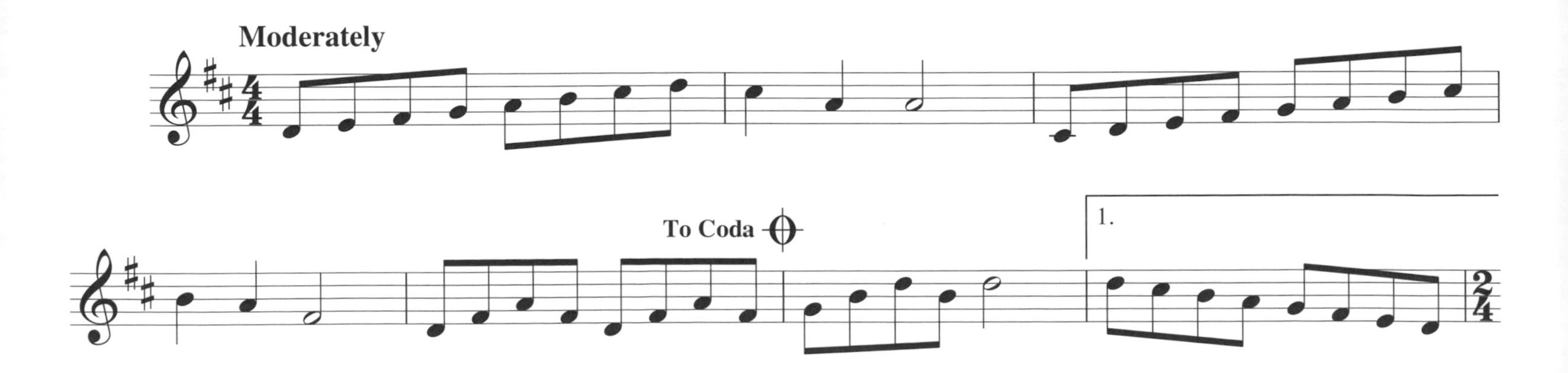

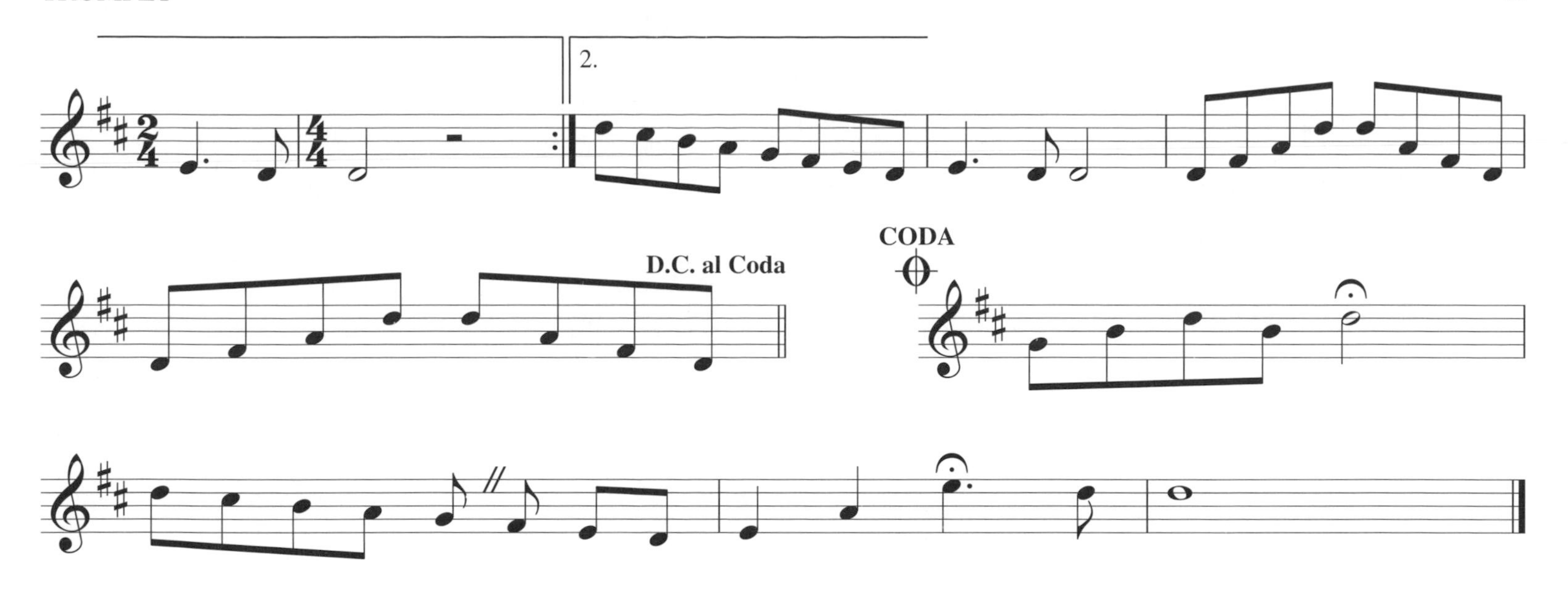

THE SECOND STAR TO THE RIGHT

from Walt Disney's PETER PAN

Words by SAMMY CAHN
Music by SAMMY FAIN

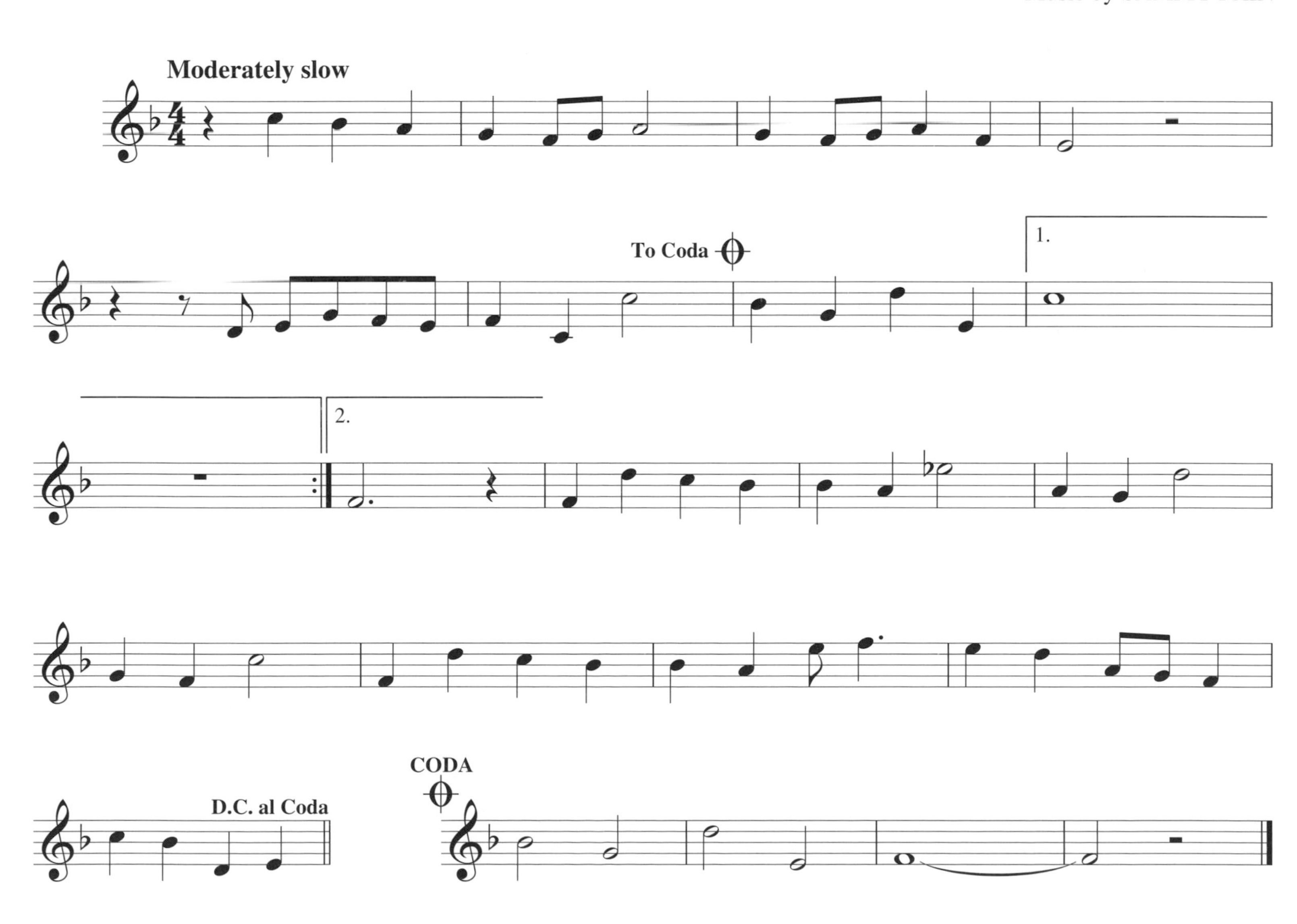

SALUDOS AMIGOS

TRUMPET

from Walt Disney's SALUDOS AMIGOS
from Walt Disney's THE THREE CABALLEROS

Words by NED WASHINGTON
Music by CHARLES WOLCOTT

TRUMPET

SO THIS IS LOVE

(The Cinderella Waltz)

from Walt Disney's CINDERELLA

Words and Music by MACK DAVID,
AL HOFFMAN and JERRY LIVINGSTON

THE SIAMESE CAT SONG

TRUMPET

from Walt Disney's LADY AND THE TRAMP

Words and Music by PEGGY LEE
and SONNY BURKE

SOONER OR LATER

from Walt Disney's SONG OF THE SOUTH

Words and Music by RAY GILBERT
and CHARLES WOLCOTT

(knock, knock)
(knock, knock)
1.
2.

SOMEDAY

TRUMPET

from Walt Disney's THE HUNCHBACK OF NOTRE DAME

Music by ALAN MENKEN
Lyrics by STEPHEN SCHWARTZ

SOMEONE'S WAITING FOR YOU

TRUMPET

from Walt Disney's THE RESCUERS

Words by CAROL CONNORS and AYN ROBBINS
Music by SAMMY FAIN

A SPOONFUL OF SUGAR

TRUMPET

from Walt Disney's MARY POPPINS

Words and Music by RICHARD M. SHERMAN
and ROBERT B. SHERMAN

THESE ARE THE BEST TIMES

TRUMPET

from Walt Disney Productions' SUPERDAD

Words and Music by
SHANE TATUM

TRUMPET

SWEET SURRENDER

from Walt Disney's THE BEARS AND I

Words and Music by
JOHN DENVER

TOYLAND MARCH

from Walt Disney's BABES IN TOYLAND

Adapted from V. HERBERT Melody
Words by MEL LEVEN
Music by GEORGE BRUNS

TRASHIN' THE CAMP

TRUMPET

from Walt Disney Pictures' TARZAN™

Words and Music by
PHIL COLLINS

WESTWARD HO, THE WAGONS!

from Walt Disney's WESTWARD HO, THE WAGONS!

Words by TOM BLACKBURN
Music by GEORGE BRUNS

SUPERCALIFRAGILISTICEXPIALIDOCIOUS

TRUMPET

from Walt Disney's MARY POPPINS

Words and Music by RICHARD M. SHERMAN
and ROBERT B. SHERMAN

THE UNBIRTHDAY SONG

TRUMPET

from Walt Disney's ALICE IN WONDERLAND

Words and Music by MACK DAVID,
AL HOFFMAN and JERRY LIVINGSTON

UNDER THE SEA

TRUMPET

from Walt Disney's THE LITTLE MERMAID

Music by ALAN MENKEN
Lyrics by HOWARD ASHMAN

1.
2.
D.S. al Coda
CODA

TRUMPET

WE'RE ALL IN THIS TOGETHER

from the Disney Channel Original Movie HIGH SCHOOL MUSICAL

Words and Music by MATTHEW GERRARD
and ROBBIE NEVIL

1.
2.
D.S. al Coda
CODA
1.
2.

WHEN SHE LOVED ME

TRUMPET

from Walt Disney Pictures' TOY STORY 2 - A Pixar Film

Music and Lyrics by
RANDY NEWMAN

WINNIE THE POOH

from Walt Disney's THE MANY ADVENTURES OF WINNIE THE POOH

Words and Music by RICHARD M. SHERMAN
and ROBERT B. SHERMAN

WHERE THE DREAM TAKES YOU

TRUMPET

from Walt Disney Pictures' ATLANTIS: THE LOST EMPIRE

Lyrics by DIANE WARREN
Music by DIANE WARREN
and JAMES NEWTON HOWARD

1.
2
2.

A WHOLE NEW WORLD

TRUMPET

from Walt Disney's ALADDIN

Music by ALAN MENKEN
Lyrics by TIM RICE

3
3
3
3

A WHALE OF A TALE

TRUMPET

from Walt Disney's 20,000 LEAGUES UNDER THE SEA

Words and Music by NORMAN GIMBEL
and AL HOFFMAN

THE WONDERFUL THING ABOUT TIGGERS

from Walt Disney's THE MANY ADVENTURES OF WINNIE THE POOH

Words and Music by RICHARD M. SHERMAN
and ROBERT B. SHERMAN

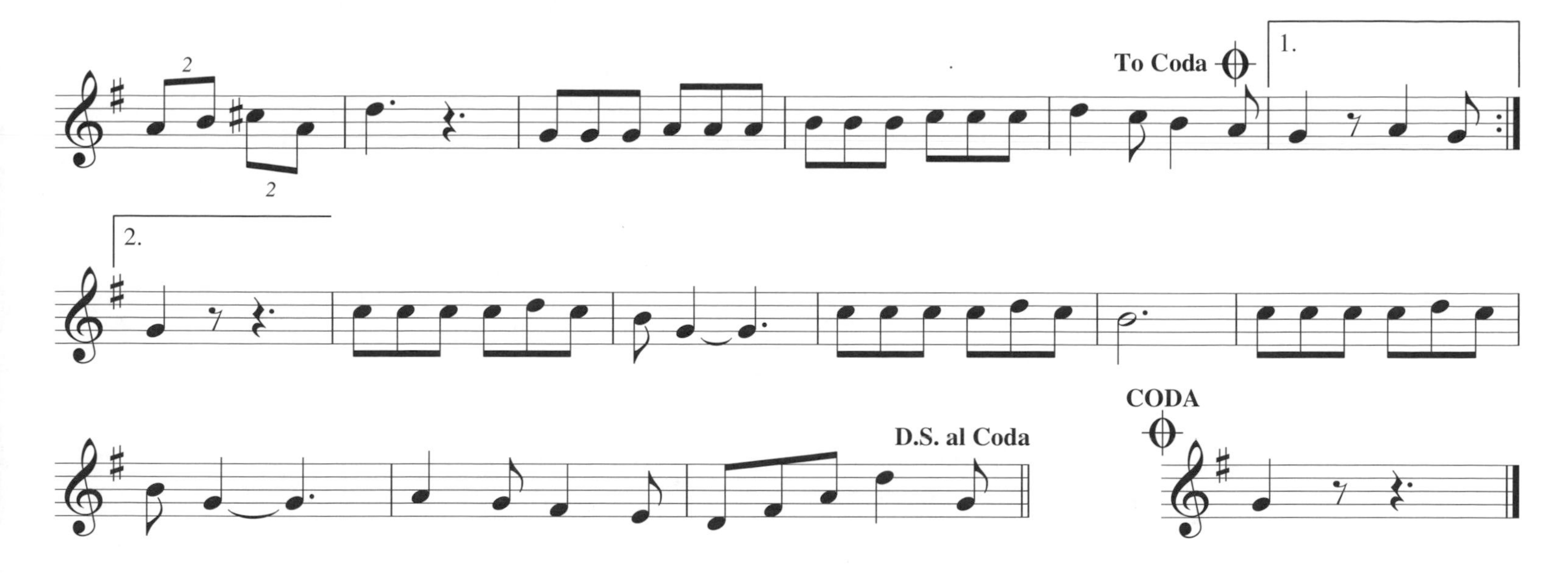

YO HO

(A Pirate's Life for Me)

from PIRATES OF THE CARIBBEAN at Disneyland Park and Magic Kingdom Park

Words by XAVIER ATENCIO
Music by GEORGE BRUNS

WRINGLE WRANGLE

(A Pretty Woman's Love)

from Walt Disney's WESTWARD HO, THE WAGONS!

TRUMPET

Words and Music by
STAN JONES

WRITTEN IN THE STARS

TRUMPET

from Elton John and Tim Rice's AIDA

Music by ELTON JOHN
Lyrics by TIM RICE

TRUMPET

YOU ARE THE MUSIC IN ME

from the Disney Channel Original Movie HIGH SCHOOL MUSICAL 2

Words and Music by
JAMIE HOUSTON

TRUMPET

YOU'LL BE IN MY HEART

(Pop Version)

from Walt Disney Pictures' TARZAN™

Words and Music by
PHIL COLLINS

CODA
1.
2.
3
3

YOU CAN FLY! YOU CAN FLY! YOU CAN FLY!

TRUMPET

from Walt Disney's PETER PAN

Words by SAMMY CAHN
Music by SAMMY FAIN

YOU'VE GOT A FRIEND IN ME

TRUMPET

from Walt Disney's TOY STORY

Music and Lyrics by
RANDY NEWMAN

ZERO TO HERO

TRUMPET

from Walt Disney Pictures' HERCULES

Music by ALAN MENKEN
Lyrics by DAVID ZIPPEL

D.C. al Coda
CODA

ZIP-A-DEE-DOO-DAH

from Walt Disney's SONG OF THE SOUTH

TRUMPET

Words by RAY GILBERT
Music by ALLIE WRUBEL